The Teacup Café

Written by Patty Farrin
Illustrated by Hilary Davis

*To Emmanuelle & Paulina 2018
Look Within — Patty Farrin*

The Teacup Café
Copyright © 2018 Patty Farrin
ISBN: 978-1-63381-143-0

All rights reserved. No part of this book may be reproduced in any form or by any means, electronic or mechanical, including photocopying, recording, or by any information storage and retrieval system, without permission in writing from the publisher.

Illustrations by Hilary Davis

Designed and produced by
Maine Authors Publishing
12 High Street
Thomaston, Maine 04861
www.maineauthorspublishing.com

Printed in the United States of America

I dedicate this book to my Mother who gave me the vision to see the beauty within at a very young age.

To my husband Rusty for your unrivaled support.

To Amy & Jac for giving me a life of purpose.

To Stephanie, Randy and Myra.
Without you, I would not have found my Teacup.

Today is Saturday, a very special day.

My mom and I are having lunch at The Teacup Café.

We go inside this dainty place and sit on comfy chairs.

We're wearing summer dresses, with flowers in our hair.

The café is so tiny, with many pretty dishes.
It is a place that's full of dreams and very special wishes.
It smells so good; it's a happy place, and I can hardly wait
to see the heart-shaped sandwiches on pretty flowered plates.

We have scones with whipped cream, a bowl full of jam.

There are tiny sandwiches made with cucumbers and ham.

There are vanilla cupcakes with colorful sprinkles.

I love how the little lights in the café twinkle.

Mom has the prettiest teacup, with roses and a vine.

I am disappointed, though, when I take a look at mine.

There are no flowers on my cup; it's as plain as it can be.

But that's okay, it will still hold a delicious cup of tea.

The sun is shining, the birds are singing. I love being with my mother.

The Teacup Café is so unique; it's unlike any other.

Every time I come here, it's such a special treat.

It's magical and delightful, with scrumptious food to eat.

We enjoy our lunch of fruit and sandwiches and drink the fragrant tea.

I cannot believe my eyes when I suddenly see

the inside of my teacup is as beautiful as can be.

With pretty pink roses encircled in a vine,

this ugly teacup is really beautiful, and for today, it is mine.

I show my mom my teacup, and she just smiles and drinks her tea,

and there in the bottom, is a golden heart, smiling back at me.

Is this a magical teacup, Mom, or, did I fail to see

something so beautiful in this dainty cup of tea?

Is the heart trying to tell me something? Is there something I should know?

If there is, will you take the time to tell me before we go?

"Sometimes, true beauty cannot be seen with the human eye.
Sometimes, we have to look with our hearts, deep down inside.

"Deep down inside of people, places, and things.
That is where true beauty lies and the happiness it can bring."

If teacups could talk, I know what mine would say.
"Please give me a chance; don't look at me that way.
Please take a look inside of me; true beauty lives in here."
I hope my message reaches you. I hope it's crystal clear.

I understood then and there what this cup was trying to say.
I took this message with me and I tucked it away!
This lesson I learned today I will never forget.
True beauty is within us, and we should never let
our eyes see what we think we see, in a certain way.
This is the lesson that I learned at The Teacup Café!

Like the teacup, the camper was not beautiful when it was purchased. It had many blemishes and rusted rims, and it needed to be painted. I could see that this little camper was really a diamond in the rough. I could see the beauty within and knew she was just perfect for me. One of the main reasons why I bought the camper was this fact: When I opened the door and was looking around, I saw a picture of an angel helping children crossing a bridge during a lightning storm. I had this same picture in my bedroom growing up! I considered this a message from my guardian angel, so I purchased the camper! Now, like the camper and the teacup, I hope children will look for the beauty *within* people, as well as everything in life that may not be beautiful to the human eye. There is beauty in everyone and everything. Sometimes you may have to look a little longer to see it. May this story remind you not to hurry, and don't worry—you are only here on earth for a little while! Take your time to see the beauty in everything and everyone. Take your time to look for the beauty within.

Written by Patty Farrin

Patty is retired from the Federal Government and is the owner of The Blue Willow Tea Room in Randolph, Maine. She is a creative baker and cook and enjoys antiques and vintage campers. She is a proud mother of two children, Amy & Jac and is married and lives with her husband Rusty in Chelsea, Maine. This is Patty's first children's book.

Illustrated by Hilary Davis

Hilary is an Augusta, Maine native who spent the majority of her young adult years painting murals for various residents and businesses. She attended Massachusetts College of Art for Fine Arts with a concentration in Costume/Fashion and completed a work-intensive fashion course at the Paris Fashion Institute. Upon graduation, she moved to New York where she interned in the theater and fashion industry. She has since moved back 'home' where she co-owns Scrummy Afters Candy Shoppe in Hallowell, Maine. This is her first time illustrating for a published work.